REVENUE SOURCING

The Retirement Planning Strategy
for the Post-Pandemic Economy

Dennis Tubbergen

Revenue Sourcing
Dennis Tubbergen

This publication is designed to provide accurate and authoritative information in regard to the subject matter covered. It is offered with the understanding that the publisher is not engaged in rendering legal, accounting, or other professional services. If legal advice or other expert assistance is required, the services of a competent professional person should be sought. The opinions expressed by the authors in this book are not endorsed by Watchdog Publishing LLC and are the sole responsibility of the author rendering the opinion.

For more information, please write:
Watchdog Publishing LLC
400 Chesterfield Center, Suite 400
Chesterfield, MO 63017

Please visit our website at: www.WatchdogPublishing.com

Table of Contents

REVENUE SOURCING

Introduction

*"Crisis, like pandemics, don't break things in and
of themselves; they show you
what's already broken."*

– Patrick Wyman

As I wrote in my best-selling book, "New Retirement Rules," in 2015, today's economy is not your Mom and Dad's economy. In that book, I warned that the Federal Reserve, the central bank of the United States, was inflating a bubble that would, at some future point, have to burst.

That bubble, as I write this, is now bursting, present tense.

Bubbles rarely unwind all at once. This one probably won't either. But it will unwind all the same.

As I will outline in this book, I believe that the volatility is just beginning, and the terrifying coronavirus situation is the pin the popped the bubble. Examining the facts and the policy response, one can only conclude that the problems are just beginning economically and financially.

And, to be frank, we are in uncharted territory here.

On the other hand, a study of history tells us that there are some eventual outcomes that are actually quite predictable.

My book, "New Retirement Rules," predicted that the bubble being inflated by the Federal Reserve after the financial crisis would eventually burst. This prediction was easy to make since a study of similar policy responses historically proved that money printing eventually leads to the same outcome every single time.

This time is no different.

The government is taking massive action in response to this situation.

The goal?

At least in part, the goal is to reflate the bubble.

A $2 trillion stimulus package has been passed; it could go to as much as $6 trillion. Mark my words, it will.

The Federal Reserve, as part of the recently

passed CARES Act, has now ceded at least some of the control of the printing press to the Washington politicians.

What could go wrong?

It doesn't matter what political party you identify with if any. Collectively speaking, politicians have never shown restraint with regard to spending. And, now, after the CARES Act, they have their collective fingers on the money creation switch.

It's nothing short of alarming, and it will make the ultimate economic and financial destination downright ugly.

I've written this book to be readable and helpful. It is my hope that you can digest and understand the new threats you're facing in one sitting as you read this short book.

My second motivation is to help you understand a tool that I believe will be vital for your future financial success – that new tool is Revenue Sourcing, and it's the title of this book.

By using Revenue Sourcing now in your own personal financial situation, you may be able to lock in your dreams of a comfortable, stress-free retirement.

But, if you continue to do things the way that you've always done them and the way that many "Wall Street Only" advisors do things, you may find yourself on the outside looking in.

This new economy requires a new approach to be successful. That's where Revenue Sourcing comes in.

Let's get started.

CHAPTER ONE
Four Lessons

*"No one cares as much about your
money as you do."*

– Dennis Tubbergen

I've been in the financial industry for a long
time, better than thirty years. And I'd like to
think I have nearly thirty years of experience, not
one year of experience repeated thirty times.

I give you my background here for reference,
not to brag.

I've been on the board of directors of investment advisory companies and broker-dealers.
I've served as President of an investment advisory company as well as a broker-dealer. I've
hosted a syndicated financial talk radio show. I
still do financial talk radio, as I've done for more
than a dozen years. I've interviewed best-selling
economic authors, top financial consultants to
business and government, and even presiden-
tial candidates. I've written six other books for

consumers on the topics of finance and economics with the goal of helping these consumers achieve success in their personal financial lives. Two of these books have achieved best-seller status on Amazon. Most importantly, my team and I continue to work with consumers who dream of retiring comfortably.

Over that time, I've learned four big lessons. I wish someone would have taught me these lessons when I started in the industry, but no one did.

This book will share these lessons with you and teach you about a new tool that you can use to navigate what's ahead economically and financially speaking.

Here's the reality. Our economy and financial system have been forever altered by recent events. Aspiring retirees who plan their financial futures using traditional means are about to see those dreams evaporate like a cool mist on a hot summer day.

On the other hand, those who dream of a comfortable, stress-free retirement can still achieve their dream by discovering the wisdom of these four, big lessons:

Here they are:

1.) No one cares as much about your money as you do.

2.) Inspect what you expect in every area of your life, but especially when it comes to your money.

3.) In every seed of adversity lies a seed of equal or greater opportunity. This lesson is laid out in the classic book by Napoleon Hill, "Think and Grow Rich." I have found it to be true over and over.

4.) If you do what everyone else does, you'll get what everyone else gets.

You can't follow the crowd when it comes to retirement planning unless you want to get the same outcome as the crowd gets. That's not a good goal. Most Americans will never realize their dream of a financially comfortable retirement.

I'm here to tell you from first-hand experience working with new clients who've followed the traditional retirement planning advice, that the traditional advice no longer works.

The sad truth is most financial professionals and stockbrokers don't utilize strategies with their clients. Strategies comprise a strategic plan to get you where you want to be at retirement while avoiding the traps that could prevent you from reaching your goal.

The scary part about today's environment is that the traps today are far, far different than just a few years ago.

Because these looming traps are so different, using a "Wall Street Only" approach by buying stocks and bonds won't work anymore.

It's blatantly obvious that we live in a boom and bust economy.

In this book, we'll discuss the reasons for this. But suffice it to say that buying the stock funds and bond funds your broker or advisor recommends and holding them is not a strategy, nor will they likely treat you well in a boom and bust economy.

Neither is buying and holding the stock and bond funds offered as part of your 401(k).

That's what the crowd does, and the crowd is almost always wrong.

Think about what a broker or advisor says when we get to the bust part of the economic cycle, and the funds in your retirement account take a beating. You probably hear things like "stay in the market for the long haul" or "you can't time the market" or "keep your eyes on the horizon."

This advice is the advice to which the crowd listens.

And, these sound bite bits of advice are certainly not strategies.

A strategy will consider all the possible alternatives and plan for them. Revenue Sourcing™, the strategy you'll discover in this book, is a strategy.

Napoleon Hill, in his classic work from the 1930s, studied the success behaviors of some of the world's brightest and most successful people. Mr. Hill was commissioned to write the book by none other than Mr. Andrew Carnegie himself.

If you've not read the book, it's a must-read.

One of the commonalities shared by the successful people interviewed by Hill for the book was their unwavering belief that "In every seed of adversity lies a seed of equal or greater opportunity."

It's true when planning for retirement too. While many aspiring retirees would see a stock market bust as an extremely adverse event, other would-be retirees see it for what it is – an opportunity provided the right strategy is in place.

In this book, you'll discover the Revenue Sourcing strategy that can create opportunities from adversity.

The next big lesson is important "inspect what you expect." Don't just assume that everything is being taken care of as you wish. You need to have check systems in place to know that your dream of a comfortable retirement is on track and is protected from threats.

I learned this the hard way.

For thirteen years in my career, I served as the President of a broker-dealer. For those of you that are not familiar with that term, a broker-dealer is a business that employs stockbrokers and financial advisors.

Part of my job as President of the company was to supervise these brokers and advisors. During that same time frame, through a consulting company, my team and I offered business and financial guidance to financial professionals.

This consulting company had more than 23,000 clients, all of whom were financial professionals. Many of these clients bought books or recordings, while others participated in coaching programs.

It was shortly before this time that the tech stock bubble collapsed. Some of you may remember that time; it was in the calendar year 2001 and 2002. As the tech stock bubble unwound and as the clients of many brokers lost money, many of these brokers told their clients some of the same things that I mentioned earlier, "stay in the market for the long haul" or "you can't time the market" or "keep your eyes on the horizon."

It was at that time that I became a very serious student of economic cycles and monetary policy. I studied dozens of books and interviewed dozens of smart economists. This intensive study is a practice that has become a way of life for me today.

That's when I began to realize that much of the financial industry doesn't use strategies. Much of the financial industry limits financial advice to only one or two financial products rather than using strategies that use all the financial tools that make sense for a client's individual situation.

I also began to realize that buy and hold investing in a boom and bust economy like ours is nothing more than gambling. And, for many hopeful retirees, using traditional retirement savings tools like IRA's and 401(k)'s can be bad.

I began to make my conclusions known to these financial professionals who were my clients.

Most were receptive.

Some were not.

One financial professional took extreme issue with my thoughts and over time found thirteen other financial professionals that agreed with him. I discovered after the fact that this financial professional recruited these other financial professionals at educational events that I would host.

This group of 14 financial professionals complained to a state agency making unfounded allegations about my consulting company.

Whenever a state agency gets a complaint, they need to investigate it. They did and saw the complaint for what it was – baseless rabble-rousing. This group then complained to a Federal agency with the same outcome.

Then, the group organized a complaint filing campaign with another US Government agency. The complaint was again investigated.

Due to the legal protocols in dealing with the government, I hired a lawyer to help answer the complaint. I provided the lawyer with the same information I had provided in answer to the complaint previously.

The lawyer assured me that everything was taken care of as I'd directed.

This brings me back to my point – always inspect what you expect.

Despite my attorney's assurances that everything had been taken care of, I got caught up in legal action with the government.

After the fact, I found out this is what happened.

After losing confidence in the attorney that I'd initially hired, I retained a different attorney. That's when I learned that the original attorney had deliberately ignored requests for information, and the government had no choice but to take legal action that could have been completely avoided had the original lawyer just done what I'd paid him to do.

The original lawyer's obvious motivation was that litigation pays a lawyer better than providing information.

Once the government's lawyer received the information, the legal action was dismissed. But only after significant expenses and lots of headaches.

Lesson learned – don't assume everything is taken care of, inspect what you expect.

Are you inspecting what you expect in your personal financial situation and in your investments?

Finally, the most important lesson of all – no one cares as much about your money as you do.

This is your money.

You earned it. You saved it. You're counting on it.

If you don't understand the strategy you're using to take care of your money, stop and take time to understand it.

If you're not even using a strategy, you need to adopt one.

This is serious stuff, and your future depends on it.

No one cares about your money as much as you do.

You're in the right place.

Revenue Sourcing is a tool that's been developed for today's economy. You're pages away from discovering a tool that can make the difference between a comfortable, stress-free retirement and a retirement that was only ever a dream.

Read on!

REVENUE SOURCING

DENNIS TUBBERGEN

CHAPTER TWO
Why Revenue Sourcing?

*"Unthinking respect for authority is the greatest
enemy of the truth."*

– Albert Einstein

The subtitle of the "New Retirement Rules"
book was "Strategies for Succeeding in the
Upcoming Economic Collapse." When this book
was released four years ago, it was met with a
great deal of skepticism from some.

Given the recent events, however, many of
these former skeptics are now converts.

Four years ago, it was tough to imagine an
economic collapse. The Fed, via quantitative
easing, had reflated the bubble that burst during
the financial crisis. It seemed that prosperity was
everywhere.

As a side note, quantitative easing is a banking term that means money printing. When you
read or hear that the Federal Reserve is "con-

ducting a program of Quantitative Easing," or the Fed is "engaging in bond purchases" or the Fed is "injecting liquidity into markets," it all means the same thing. The Fed is printing money.

Many of you reading this are undoubtedly familiar with the Federal Reserve and how it operates. Some of you, however, may not be acquainted with how the central bank functions.

In order to fully understand why Revenue Sourcing is the tool you need to use now to lock in your retirement dreams, you need to have a general understanding as to how the Federal Reserve and the banking system works.

In short - it ain't pretty.

Henry Ford, many decades ago, observed, "It is well enough that people of the nation do not understand our banking and monetary system, for if they did, I believe there would be a revolution before tomorrow morning."

Since Mr. Ford made that comment, the banking system has not improved, it's only gotten worse.

The Federal Reserve Act was passed in 1913 and signed into law by President Woodrow Wilson on December 23 as congress was recessing for the holidays.

The Federal Reserve Act gave private bankers control of the monetary policy of the United States. You read that correctly. Private bankers have controlled US monetary policy for over 100 years.

Let me ask you to consider a commonsense question – do you think the group of private bankers that comprise the Federal Reserve have your best interests ahead of their own?

Prior to the formation of the Federal Reserve, the US Dollar was backed fully by gold. In fact, up until 1933, one-ounce gold coins circulated as currency. They were worth $20 and were called twenty-dollar gold pieces.

During World War I, many countries around the globe abandoned the gold standard in order to print money to fund the war. However, after the war, in 1919, the US returned to a gold exchange standard. The gold exchange standard allowed anyone possessing a paper bill to exchange it for gold. If you were a creditor, you could even require your debtor to make payment to you in gold rather than in paper.

At this point in US history, gold was money as it has been for most of recorded history.

When the Great Depression hit, largely due to the Federal Reserve printing money and creating debt excesses, the stock market crashed.

After the stock market crash, there was a rush to hoard gold since people didn't trust financial institutions anymore. Many large banks failed, and then-President Franklin Roosevelt declared a bank holiday which relieved bankers of any obligation to honor the deposits of their customers.

The bank holiday was declared in March of 1933, and by April, President Roosevelt issued an executive order that required all Americans to turn in their gold. The government 'bought' the gold from citizens by giving them freshly printed paper currency.

Hardly a fair trade.

But there were stiff penalties for not complying with the government mandate to turn in your gold, including imprisonment.

By January 1934, the Gold Reserve Act was passed. It prohibited the private ownership of gold unless you had a license. This allowed for massive dollar devaluation and allowed the Federal Reserve to print money.

By 1944, after World War II, as part of the Bretton Woods agreement, the US Dollar was made the reserve currency of the world. While US citizens could not legally own gold, any foreign bank or other entity possessing US Dollars could exchange them for gold at the rate of $35 per ounce.

The dollar was the most desirable currency in the world as it could be exchanged for gold at any time. As a result, nearly all international trade took place in US Dollars.

This made the US Dollar the 'reserve' currency of the world. Any nation that wanted to trade with other nations inventoried or "reserved" US Dollars to do so.

This system began to unravel in the 1960s with massive US Government spending.

The 1960s saw the expensive Vietnam War, the birth of the federal Medicare and Medicaid programs, and the War on Poverty.

Regardless of your political leanings, we can all agree that the war and these programs were expensive and consumed a lot more money than the Federal Government collected in tax revenues.

The politicians and policymakers had the same three choices to deal with the deficit spending as today's politicians have:

1.) Raise taxes

2.) Cut spending

3.) Print currency

Predictably, the politicians of the 1960s elected to turn on the money-printing machine.

It didn't take long for foreign investors and banks to get nervous. They saw how much money was being created and decided that they'd prefer the gold that backed the dollars to the paper dollars. Certainly, you and I would have made the same decision.

The reality is that the US had printed far more in paper currency than the country had gold to back.

As foreign demands to exchange their US Dollars for gold intensified, President Richard Nixon closed the gold window. In 1971, he went on television and stated that he was temporarily suspending the redemptions of US Dollars for gold.

During his televised speech, Mr. Nixon offered this explanation on the suspension of US Dollars for gold (emphasis added)

We must protect the position of the American dollar as a pillar of monetary stability around the world.

In the past seven years, there has been an average of one international monetary crisis every year. Now, who gains from these crises? Not the working man, not the investor, not the real producers of wealth. **The gainers are the international money speculators.** *Because they thrive on crises, they help to create them.*

In recent weeks, **the speculators have been waging an all-out war on the American dollar.** *The strength of a nation's currency is based on the strength of that nation's economy – and the American economy is by far the strongest in the world. Accordingly, I have directed the Secretary of the Treasury to take action necessary to defend the dollar against the speculators.*

I have directed Secretary Connally **to suspend temporarily the convertibility of the American dolla***r except in amounts and conditions determined to be in the interest of monetary stability and in the best interests of the United States.*

Now, what is this action – which is very technical – what does it mean for you? **Let me lay to rest the bugaboo of what is called devaluation.**

*If you want to buy a foreign car or take a trip abroad, market conditions may cause your dollar to buy slightly less. But if you are among the overwhelming majority of Americans who buy American-made products in America, **your dollar will be worth just as much tomorrow as it is today.***

The effect of this action, in other words, will be to stabilize the dollar.

Now, this action will not win us any friends among the international money traders. But our primary concern is with the American workers, and with fair competition around the world.

*To our friends abroad, including the many responsible members of the international banking community who are dedicated to stability and the flow of trade, I give this assurance: The United States has always been and will continue to be, a forward-looking and trustworthy trading partner. In full cooperation with the International Monetary Fund and those who trade with us, **we will press for the necessary reforms to set up an urgently needed new international monetary system.** Stability and equal treatment are in everybody's best interest. I am determined that the American dollar must never again be a hostage in the hands of international speculators.*

In that speech, Mr. Nixon followed every rule of politics.

Rule number one: never blame yourself.

Rule number two: seem sincere about a solution even when it's blatantly obvious you're not sincere.

Rule number three: tell people what they want to hear.

The "international money speculators" that Mr. Nixon demonized in his speech were foreign investors and banks that were exchanging their US Dollars for gold as they were entitled to do under the Bretton Woods agreement. These "international money speculators" were not taking advantage of the United States, as Mr. Nixon suggested, it was quite the opposite. The United States changed the deal and did so arbitrarily.

While Mr. Nixon stated in his speech that this was a temporary measure, it was permanent. Those redemptions of the US Dollar for gold have never resumed.

Then Mr. Nixon told a whopper so big, even Pinocchio would have blushed. Nixon stated his actions would not result in dollar devaluation and that his action would stabilize the US Dollar.

Hardly.

In 1971, the average sale price of a home in the US was about $24,000. The price of gold was $35 per ounce. It took about 685 ounces of gold to buy the average new home.

Today, as of this writing, gold is about $1700 per ounce. The average new home costs approximately $320,000. That means that the same 685 ounces of gold would buy about 3.5 new homes.

Since that day in 1971, the US Dollar has been hugely devalued, and the trend is now strengthening exponentially.

Since the US Dollar was no longer backed by gold, the primary reason that foreign investors would want to hold US Dollars had disappeared.

A new plan was needed to create demand for US Dollars.

Nixon, with input from his advisors, including Henry Kissinger, came up with a plan to get the oil-producing world to sell all their oil in US Dollars. Recognizing that the worldwide demand for oil was going to increase, if all the world's primary oil producers required that sales of oil take place in US Dollars, then any oil-consuming country would need US Dollars to get the oil they needed.

The Nixon administration cut the oil for dollars deal with Saudi Arabia in 1973, promising military favors and protection in exchange. By 1975, every OPEC country was selling oil in US Dollars.

The Petro-Dollar was born.

The Petro-Dollar is now weakening. Many oil-producing countries over the past several years have moved to accept payment in other currencies.

This topic is a book in and of itself.

Back to the Federal Reserve.

The "Fed" is still the central bank of the United States. It is still controlled by private bankers who make the 'money rules.'

Up until the financial crisis of 2008, the Fed would control the money supply by setting interest rates and reserve requirements.

Bankers under Federal Reserve rules have to reserve 10% of a bank customer's deposit. If you made a deposit into your bank account of $100,000, your banker would reserve 10%

or $10,000 and could then loan the remaining $90,000 to another bank customer.

Under this system, the more borrowing that takes place, the more money is created.

Here's an example to make the point clear. You make your $100,000 deposit. Your banker reserves the required 10% and loans out the other $90,000 to a bank customer who wants to buy a piece of property.

The seller of the property receives the $90,000 payment and deposits it in her bank account. Her banker reserves 10% or $9,000 and loans out the remaining 90% or $81,000.

As long as borrowing continues, the original $100,000 bank deposit results in $1,000,000 of new money with a 10% reserve requirement.

If the Fed wants to jump-start the economy, the Federal Reserve Board reduces interest rates to encourage borrowing. More borrowing means more money is created.

More money creation means asset bubbles form. When studying history, there is one eternal truth about asset bubbles – they burst 100% of the time.

When asset bubbles burst, the Fed attempts to reflate the bubble by reducing interest rates.

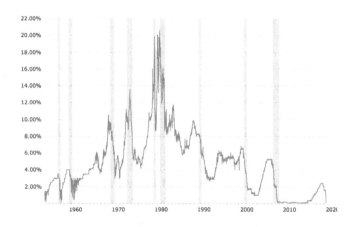

This chart is a chart of interest rates set by the Federal Reserve. Notice that from 1980 to the present, interest rates have generally been declining, which means money has been created.

As interest rates dropped from the late 1980s to the early 1990s, money was created, and the tech stock bubble formed. The bubble burst, and the stock market crashed.

The response of the Federal Reserve was to reduce interest rates in order to create more money. Notice that in the early 2000s interest rates fell to about 1%.

The result, as you undoubtedly remember, was a housing bubble and a stock market bubble that predictably crashed. The response to the crash was just as predictable – the Fed reduced interest rates to 0%.

This time though, the bubble wasn't reflating.

Why?

A little critical thinking gives us the answer.

When money is loaned into existence, more money creation can only happen if the economy has the capacity for more debt. When the economy has collectively reached its debt limit, reducing interest rates to loan more money into existence will not work.

A desperate Fed had to come up with a new plan.

The Fed decided that if consumers weren't going to borrow money, they would print it and get it into the economy. They would do this via a process they dubbed "quantitative easing."

According to the Fed, this extreme monetary policy of creating money out of thin air would, like Nixon's suspension of US Dollars for gold, be only "temporary."

The Fed would print money and then use that newly created money to buy assets from member banks.

The law stated that the Fed could only buy government-backed assets from member banks, so the Fed began to purchase US Government debt like Treasury bills, notes, and bonds as well as government-backed mortgage securities.

By 2010, the Fed was printing what seemed like an outrageous amount of "temporary" money. This from "CNN Money" On November 3, 2010 (Source: https://money.cnn.com/2010/11/03/news/economy/fed_decision/index.htm) (emphasis added):

In its latest move to jump-start the sluggish recovery, the Federal Reserve announced it would pump billions into the economy.

The central bank will buy $600 billion in long-term Treasuries over the next eight months, *the Fed said Wednesday.*

$600 billion divided by eight months equals $75 billion per month. More from the article (emphasis added):

The Fed has already kept the federal funds rate, a benchmark for interest rates on a variety of consumer and business loans, at historic lows near zero since December 2008. The Fed said Wednesday that it would continue to hold the rate at "exceptionally low levels" for an "extended period."

The federal funds rate is the central bank's key tool to spur the economy, and a low rate is thought to encourage spending by making it cheaper to borrow money.

When already low rates failed to get consumers and businesses to spend, the Fed decided to resort to the more unconventional tool of quantitative easing.

*But critics of QE2, including some Fed members, believe that too much monetary stimulus might lead to runaway inflation that could derail the economy **or future asset bubbles that could endanger economic stability over the long term.***

The most outspoken voting member of the Fed, Kansas City Fed President Thomas Hoenig, was once again the lone dissent among policymakers, saying he believed the risks of additional securities purchases outweighed the benefits.

*Other opponents have argued that it simply won't work. **The Fed already made nearly $2 trillion in similar purchases during the***

Great Recession, and current low-interest rates have not jolted spending, they say.

*"I don't think this is going to make any dif-ference at all," said Paul Ashworth, senior U.S. economist with Capital Economics, who feels the plan is too small. **"This is a slippery slope. Once you're on it, it's very hard to get off."***

He predicts a repeat of what happened with the first round of quantitative easing two years ago. The Fed initially announced a $600 bil-lion program in November 2008, but then four months later, increased that to $1.8 trillion when it wasn't enough.

That article is from about ten years ago.

In prior books, including "Economic Con-sequences" in 2011 and the best-selling "New Retirement Rules" in 2015, I predicted that this new Fed money printing policy would continue until the financial system blew up and a reset occurred.

It seems that we are on that path. What began as a program that was temporary now appears like it is here to stay with the numbers getting ever larger.

The CARES Act, recently passed in response to the coronavirus situation, expands the power of the Fed to print money and, alarmingly, gives money printing discretion to the US Treasury.

Jim Bianco, of Bianco Research, commented on these new powers in a "Bloomberg" opinion piece (Source: https://finance.yahoo.com/news/feds-cure-risks-being-worse-110052807.html) (emphasis added):

But it's the alphabet soup of new programs that deserve special consideration, as they could have profound long-term consequences for the functioning of the Fed and the allocation of capital in financial markets. Specifically, these are:

CPFF (Commercial Paper Funding Facility) – buying commercial paper from the issuer.

PMCCF (Primary Market Corporate Credit Facility) – buying corporate bonds from the issuer.

TALF (Term Asset-Backed Securities Loan Facility) – funding backstop for asset-backed securities.

SMCCF (Secondary Market Corporate Credit Facility) – buying corporate bonds and bond ETFs in the secondary market.

MSBLP (Main Street Business Lending Program) – Details are to come, but it will lend to eligible small and medium-sized businesses, complementing efforts by the Small Business Association.

To put it bluntly, the Fed isn't allowed to do any of this. The central bank is only allowed to purchase or lend against securities that have a government guarantee. *This includes Treasury securities, agency mortgage-backed securities and the debt issued by Fannie Mae and Freddie Mac. An argument can be made that can also include municipal securities,* **but nothing in the laundry list above.**

So how can they do this?

The Fed will finance a special purpose vehicle (SPV) for each acronym to conduct these operations. The Treasury, using the Exchange Stabilization Fund, will make an equity investment in each SPV and be in a "first loss" position.

What does this mean?

In essence, the Treasury, not the Fed, is buying all these securities and backstopping of loans; the Fed is acting as banker and providing financing. *The Fed hired BlackRock Inc. to purchase these securities and handle the administration of the SPVs on behalf of the owner, the Treasury.*

In other words, the federal government is nationalizing large swaths of the financial markets. *The Fed is providing the money to do it. BlackRock will be making the trades.*

This scheme essentially merges the Fed and Treasury into one organization. So, meet your new Fed chairman, Donald J. Trump.

In 2008 when something similar was done, it was on a smaller scale. Since few understood it, the Bush and Obama administrations ceded total control of those acronym programs to then-Fed Chairman Ben Bernanke. He unwound them at the first available opportunity. But now, 12 years later, we have a much better understanding of how they work. And we have a president who has made it very clear how displeased he is that central bankers haven't used their considerable power to force the Dow Jones Industrial Average at least 10,000 points higher, something he has complained about many times before the pandemic hit.

When the Fed was rightly alarmed by the current dysfunction in the fixed-income markets, they felt they needed to act. This was the correct thought. But, to get the authority to stabilize these "private" markets, central bankers needed the Treasury to agree to

nationalize (own) them so they could provide the funds to do it.

In effect, the Fed is giving the Treasury access to its printing press. This means that, in the extreme, the administration would be free to use its control, not the Fed's control, of these SPVs to instruct the Fed to print more money so it could buy securities and hand out loans in an effort to ramp financial markets higher going into the election. *Why stop there? Should Trump win re-election, he could try to use these SPVs to get those 10,000 Dow Jones points he feels the Fed has denied everyone.*

What this means is that moving ahead, the rules have changed.

The US Treasury will invest in the SPV, which will invest in commercial paper and corporate bonds. Where will the Treasury get the money to do this?

From the Federal Reserve.

Where will the Federal Reserve get the money?

They will create it. Out of thin air.

As I stated ten years ago, when the money printing began, this is a slippery slope. Once money printing begins, history teaches us it never stops. Over time it just becomes more extreme; more and more money is created until it doesn't produce the desired outcome, and a reset occurs.

Since this provision of the stimulus package virtually ensures that more money printing will occur, look for the continued devaluation of the US Dollar over time. And, look for more crashes in traditional assets.

And, don't expect the real inflation numbers to be reflected in the official inflation rate. But, watch the nominal cost of tangible assets; that's where you'll see evidence of the inflation.

The question is this – will the Fed be able to reflate the bubble?

No one knows for sure.

That's where Revenue Sourcing comes in.

It protects you from the next bubble bursting and from the inflation that will eventually arrive.

Revenue Sourcing Resource

Visit www.Revenue-Sourcing.com
for additional Revenue Sourcing resources.

Our team hosts periodic, free webinars on how you can use Revenue Sourcing to achieve your dream of a comfortable, stress-free retirement. Also, on the website, you'll find resources to help you build your own Revenue Sourcing map and your own Revenue Sourcing Allocation Plan. You will also find resources to help you maximize the benefits you'll receive from Social Security and be able to request a free fee and drawdown analysis as described in this book.

REVENUE SOURCING

CHAPTER THREE

Revenue Sourcing; Because History Tells Us Where We Go From Here

"History teaches us that men and nations behave wisely once they have exhausted all other alternatives."

– Abba Eban

I need to apologize to my history teacher.

When he first told me that those who don't study history are doomed to repeat it, I was a young, dismissive student.

But, now that I've become a serious student of financial and economic history, he was right.

Based on the current policy response, it seems that most of the world has shunned the lessons offered by history when it comes to things financial and economic.

While this topic could consume volumes, in the interest of brevity, I will provide you with enough historical background to demonstrate to you the importance of Revenue Sourcing when doing your planning.

Bubbles and busts have been taking place for thousands of years.

Why?

Because human behavior is quite predictable.

The political response to bubbles is even more predictable because the collective behavior of groups of politicians is predictable to an even greater extent.

A study of history reveals the cycle:

1.) A sound money system is used for commerce.

2.) A policy of sound money is weakened as politicians over-promise and need to fund those promises. As I mentioned previously, politicians have only three options to deal with deficits that emerge as a result of overpromising:

a. Raise taxes

b. Cut spending

c. Print currency

3.) Eventually, the temptation to yield to printing currency is too hard to resist, and money creation usually begins as a temporary measure.

4.) Temporary always becomes permanent, and money creation grows exponentially.

5.) Money creation creates a series of bubbles and busts, with each subsequent bust worse than the prior bust.

6.) Eventually, money creation doesn't work, and the currency is destroyed by massive currency devaluation. Inflation is rampant.

7.) A reset occurs, and a sound money system is adopted.

There are countless historical examples of this cycle repeating. That's why Revenue Sourcing is critical in today's environment. You need to be protected from the bust part of the cycle, and the rampant inflation that history teaches us is inevitable.

We'll review just a couple of historical examples.

John Law was France's central banker in the

early 1700s. As you now know, a central banker controls a central bank that can print currency virtually out of thin air.

Mr. Law was not French but Scottish, having been born in Edinburgh in 1671. He was born into the money business, as his father was a successful banker and goldsmith. Mr. Law began working in these trades as an apprentice at the age of fourteen, and, at the age of seventeen, began working full time in the family business when his father suddenly passed away.

Mr. Law was always popular with the ladies, and now with his family's estate under his control, set off for London, where he learned how to be a successful gambler, which was not a surprising decision for a wealthy seventeen-year-old.

Unfortunately for Law, his gambling and womanizing led to him being challenged to a duel, which he accepted. Law won the duel, killing his challenger. As a result of his role in the duel, Law was sentenced to be hanged; however, with some help from some friends in high places, he managed to escape the death penalty during the appeals process.

Law escaped to Paris where, for the next several years, he made his living gambling. As a result of this gambling lifestyle, he began to have regular contact with the Duc d' Orleans, who was also an avid gambler.

Even though Law lived a high-roller kind of life, there were some signs that Law wanted to do more with his life; he wanted to be more significant. Law began to publish some serious pieces on economics and became very interested in the financing of trade. During their gambling sessions, Law had the ear of the Duc who enjoyed listening to Law's views on trade and finance.

At about this same time, Louis XIV of France was dying.

While Louis was a popular king while he reigned, after his death, he left a mixed legacy due to the size of the national debt that he left to his heir, Louis XV, who was only seven years old at the time he took the throne.

Due to the new king's young age, the Duc d' Orleans was appointed as regent. The first and most pressing problem that the newly appointed regent faced was the huge amount of debt accumulated by the now-deceased king.

The Duc made the same decision politicians have made for centuries—he decided to print currency.

Because paper currency was not yet in use at the time, the Duc printed currency by debasing the coins used as currency. Newly minted coins were created with 20% less precious metal content than previously issued coins.

This was the eighteenth-century equivalent of currency printing. French citizens, recognizing that the older coins were more valuable, began to hoard them. In response, the state passed a law that made hoarding the old coins illegal and punishable by imprisonment. There were also rewards offered to those who blew the whistle on coin hoarders.

Economically speaking, things were going south in a hurry, and that's when John Law arrived on the scene. The Duc granted Law a bank and put him charge of the management of royal revenues.

Law was also given the authority to issue paper currency. The paper currency would be secured by the royal revenues and the land owned by the kingdom.

Law's bank began to print paper currency.

Initially, Law guaranteed that the paper currency could be exchanged for coins comprised of precious metal. These coins were being issued at the same time the paper currency was introduced. Both coins and paper currency circulated.

But it didn't take long for the paper currency to become more popular than the coins that were circulating because the paper currency was more convenient to use than the coins.

By introducing the paper currency in this manner, Law was able to pull most of the coins containing precious metals out of circulation, leaving mostly paper currency circulating. Law calculated that printing more currency would help get the French economy moving again.

The money printing created a climate of prosperity, or so it seemed.

The currency printing continued.

Paris was booming.

High-end luxury items were sold before they hit the shelves. Real estate values went through the roof. Rents skyrocketed, and the stock market just kept on rising. Shares in the famed Mississippi Company increased over 1,900% in just one year!

A bubble had been created the same way that bubbles are always created through easy credit and easy money. Yet, in the midst of a bubble, few recognized that the bubble existed.

The Duc saw what prosperity had been created through the printing of currency, and he was a happy guy. He reasoned that if some currency printing had produced these results, then more currency printing would produce even better results.

The Duc went over Law's head and ordered more currency printing.

However, as also always happens, some of the smarter French citizens began to get nervous due to the large amount of currency printing. One of the first of the French citizens to take action was a nobleman who sent three wagon-loads of paper currency to Law's bank to demand payment in the coins containing precious metals.

This was enough to allow some of the other smart Frenchmen to see the light; this paper currency system was highly suspect, and the speculative bubble may be close to bursting.

More and more French citizens started to cash in their paper currency, exchanging it for coins. Some smart French citizens, fearing the government, began to ship coins, bullion, and jewels to other countries.

The run on the bank for the coins containing precious metals continued, forcing the French parliament to take action.

The parliament issued a law that stated that the coins would carry only 95% of the value of the paper currency. It didn't work. The public didn't buy it, and the run on the bank for coins continued.

Law had no choice but to abolish coins as a medium of exchange.

The French currency was now a fiat currency since the link between paper currency, and precious metals were eliminated. Law, in the early eighteenth century, did what President Nixon did in 1971 when the US dollar became a fiat currency.

Law also made it illegal to own gold (like Franklin Roosevelt would do later in the US during the Great Depression). He closed borders and sent instructions to coach houses to refuse fresh horses to anyone traveling out of the country until their bags were inspected. There were substantial fines for violating these rules, and these fines were shared with the whistleblowers who informed the authorities about these violations.

It wasn't long before the French monetary system collapsed, making Law the most hated man in France. Fortunately for him, he escaped to the city of Venice.

Gold and silver were once again used in commerce after the bubble burst, and it would be eighty years before the French introduced paper currency again.

The historical cycle is clear, as noted above.

1.) A sound money system is used for commerce.

2.) A policy of sound money is weakened as politicians over-promise and need to fund those promises. As I mentioned previously, politicians have only three options to deal with deficits that emerge as a result of overpromising:

a. Raise taxes

b. Cut spending

c. Print currency

3.) Eventually, the temptation to yield to printing currency is too hard to resist, and money creation usually begins as a temporary measure.

4.) Temporary always becomes permanent, and money creation grows exponentially.

5.) Money creation creates a series of bubbles and busts, with each subsequent bust worse than the prior bust.

6.) Eventually, money creation doesn't work, and the currency is destroyed by massive currency devaluation. Inflation is rampant.

7.) A reset occurs, and a sound money system is adopted.

Let's look at the case of Weimar, Germany, after World War I.

Germany hoped that it would quickly win the war and reap the bounty from the nations it conquered, which, to the government, justified the use of the printing press to fund the war. (Notice how the money printing was intended to be temporary? It never is.)

It didn't take too long for this currency printing to create inflation; however, during the war, the German government used extensive propaganda to attempt to hide the inflation from the population, and it censored information heavily.

Every German stock exchange was closed for the duration of the war, so the effect of Reichsbank (the German central bank that was printing money) policies on stocks was unknown. Further, foreign exchange rates were not published, and only those in contact with neutral markets, such as Amsterdam or Zurich, could guess what was going on. Only when the war was over, when censorship stopped, did it become clear to all that Germany had already met an economic disaster nearly as ugly as her military one.

Due to the bad economy, many German soldiers began to desert the military. A German newspaper attributed Germany's loss of the war partly to the fact that men were abandoning the front to return home and support their families. With rapidly rising inflation, it was impossible to make ends meet on military pay.

To make things worse, the Treaty of Versailles, which ended the war, imposed massive reparations on Germany. The payment demands made of Germany were so large that Germany could never realistically pay with "honest" money.

The implications of these demands for the German economy were enormous. The German army had to be reduced to 25% of its size, which meant that over 250,000 men were suddenly added to the labor force, increasing the rate of unemployment. The central bank began massive currency printing to attempt to stimulate the economy and bring down the unemployment rate.

Inflation set in.

By September 1920, prices were twelve times as high as they had been before the war.

By the autumn of 1920, the strains on the economy in the wake of the war were apparent, but employment was still fairly strong. Nevertheless, prices were rising as a direct result of this money printing.

Food had accounted for half the family budget immediately after the war, but now nearly three-quarters of any family's income was spent on groceries. The food for a family of four persons, which cost 60 marks a week in April 1919, cost 198 marks by September 1920, and 230 marks by November 1920. Certain items, such as lard, ham, tea, and eggs, rose to between thirty and forty times the prewar price. On the bright side, in contrast to Austria, the official unemployment figure was low, and only 375,000 people were on the dole.

Faced with a bill, it could not pay from a war it could not afford, Germany continued to print money at an even faster pace.

Bankers from Switzerland, Italy, and Germany concluded that it was impossible for Germany to continue her reparation payments and that, sooner or later, she would have to declare herself bankrupt, followed (they thought) by France and then Italy. The mark, at 310 to the British pound in mid-August, had sped downward to over 400 by mid-September and was still going down.

Germans everywhere were doing everything they could to convert their marks into other currencies. Goods were flying off the shelves of shops as people tried to protect themselves against the falling value of the currency.

By the end of 1921, workers had lost so much faith in the government that many just stopped voting. The economic hardships brought about by inflation were evident in everyday prices.

Owners of large industrial conglomerates benefited from the inflation, so they constantly reminded the populace that amid the economic chaos, employment was still very high.

It didn't take long for the cost of basic staples to become out of reach for German consumers as the mark plunged.

A liter of milk, which had cost seven marks in April 1922 and 16 marks in August, cost 26 marks by mid-September. And beer had climbed from 5.60 marks a liter to 18 and then to 30. A single egg, 3.60 marks in April, now cost nine marks. In only nine months, the weekly bill for an identical food basket had risen from 370 marks to 2,615.

The soaring inflation led to currency chaos, and many entities began to issue their own forms of money.

Large industrial concerns began to pay their workmen partly in notes and partly in coupons of their own, which were accepted by local tradesmen on the understanding that they would be redeemed within a very short time.

Cities also started to issue their own currencies, aware that any delay in receiving their pay packets would dangerously aggravate workers, whose main concern was to spend them before they depreciated.

At 35,000 to the pound at Christmas in 1922, the mark fell, and at the end of January 1923, it touched 227,500, which was well over 50,000 to the dollar.

At the end of September of 1923, the German Chancellor declared a state of emergency and put Germany under military rule.

Finally, in November of 1923, the German government took action to stabilize the currency. The German government set up the Rentenbank to issue a new currency, the Rentenmark, which would be backed by land and industrial goods. The Rentenmark finally stabilized the German currency.

There are many, many other examples of historical money printing. While these incidents have occurred at different times and in different countries, they all have one thing in common. Once money printing starts, it's NEVER temporary.

And, it only works until it doesn't.

That's where Revenue Sourcing comes in.

Revenue Sourcing Resources

Visit www.Revenue-Sourcing.com
for additional Revenue Sourcing resources.

Our team hosts periodic, free webinars on how you can use Revenue Sourcing to achieve your dream of a comfortable, stress-free retirement. Also, on the website, you'll find resources to help you build your own Revenue Sourcing map and your own Revenue Sourcing Allocation Plan. You will also find resources to help you maximize the benefits you'll receive from Social Security and be able to request a free fee and drawdown analysis as described in this book.

REVENUE SOURCING

CHAPTER FOUR
Why You Should Be Revenue Sourcing

"We cannot solve our problems with the same thinking we used when we created them."

– Albert Einstein

The historical currency cycle outlined in the last chapter has repeated itself time and time again. From the Roman Empire to the present, politicians and policymakers have ultimately resorted to money printing to attempt to "paper over" financial problems.

As we've discussed, this creates a series of boom and bust cycles that repeat until confidence is ultimately lost in the currency, at which point a reset occurs.

This pattern is repeating itself once again.

But the world is radically different today than at any time in the past.

Presently, EVERY currency in the world is a

fiat currency meaning there is no backing of any world currency by anything tangible like gold or silver. This is the first time in recorded monetary history that we've been at the end of this historical money cycle with zero currencies that have a link to something tangible.

The last world currency to eliminate the link to gold was the Swiss Franc in 2000. Prior to that date, the Swiss Franc was backed 40% by gold.

Here is why that is important.

EVERY world central bank can now print currency. That has allowed the present bubble to reach levels never before seen.

The last time we reached the end of this historical currency cycle in the US was 1929. At that time, the US Dollar, as well as other world currencies, had at least some gold backing.

So, the big question is this?

Will the Federal Reserve through money creation be able to reflate the bubble again?

No one knows the answer to that question.

We are truly in uncharted territory here.

Let me also be clear, should the Fed be successful reflating the bubble, we don't know how long it will be until the next bust.

Japan hit the ultimate bust years ago and has responded by printing money. The country has never recovered.

I understand that as an aspiring retiree, it would be nice to have someone be able to tell you what is going to happen and when it will happen. But again, this is uncharted territory.

No one can tell you the "when."

But here is what I can tell you.

You have two very real risks, and you will most assuredly have to deal with them both in the future.

One, the current bubble continues to unravel further devastating the value of the 401(k) and IRA plans of millions of Americans. Or, perhaps the Fed reflates the bubble, and you experience this in the ultimate bust at some future point rather than currently.

In either outcome, following the traditional Wall Street Advisor approach of investing in stock fund and bonds funds, you will fail in my view.

Two, in an effort to reflate the bubble through money creation, we see massive inflation or even hyperinflation, as noted in the last chapter.

You have two risks. One, a bust, devastates the value of your assets. Two, money printing means your assets no longer buy what they used to buy.

That's where Revenue Sourcing comes in.

Revenue Sourcing is a tool developed for today's unique environment to allow you to identify and lock in future retirement revenues and then protect these future revenues from future inflation.

Revenue Sourcing is a process that can ensure a comfortable, stress-free retirement no matter what markets do.

Here are the Revenue Sourcing steps:

1.) Identify the level of retirement income needed or desired.

2.) Identify when the income will be needed.

3.) Build the Revenue Sourcing Map. Include Social Security income, pension income, earned income, business income, and income from investments.

4.) Once the Revenue Sourcing Map is built, adjust allocations, and do long-term tax management.

Let's review the steps in detail.

Step One. Identify the level of retirement income you desire. Many people who dream of a comfortable retirement don't quantify the dream.

What do I mean by quantifying the dream?

You need to know exactly how much retirement income you want to have.

If you don't know, relax. You're in good company.

While there are many different "rules of thumb" to use when determining how much income you'll need during retirement. I've found that most of these guides are unrealistic.

One such rule of thumb suggests you'll need 2/3rd's of the income you have now when you retire. I've found that to be totally unrealistic.

Who wants to retire and have less income and more time on their hands?

More expendable time typically means more opportunities to spend money. When in doubt as to how much income you'll need during retirement, assume you want to replace your current level of income.

Step Two. Identify when the income will be needed. When do you want to retire?

If you're unsure, you are once again in good company. Some people want to retire as soon as possible. Others don't ever plan on retiring; they simply have a dream of being financially independent. Still, others are just beginning to consider the options and the possibilities.

If you are unsure, determine the earliest date you would retire and do your revenue sourcing from that date. Working past that date simply makes your Revenue Sourcing model work that much better.

Step Three: Build the Revenue Sourcing Map. The first two steps of the Revenue Sourcing process are big picture items – how much income do you want, and when do you want it.

As the old saying goes, the devil is in the details. That's where the third step of the Revenue Sourcing process comes in – building the Revenue Sourcing map. The Revenue Sourcing map is the blueprint that will determine if your dreams are realistic and achievable.

The Revenue Sourcing map takes these factors into account:

1.) How to maximize Social Security benefits

2.) Incorporating any pension benefits

3.) Including any earned or business income anticipated

4.) Including any real estate related income like net rental income, land contract income or rent-to-own investment income

5.) Additional income needed from investments to meet your income desires

Once you've determined these factors, then it's time to make an allocation adjustment. More on this momentarily.

Revenue Sourcing Resources

Visit www.Revenue-Sourcing.com
for additional Revenue Sourcing resources.

Our team hosts periodic, free webinars on how you can use Revenue Sourcing to achieve your dream of a comfortable, stress-free retirement. Also, on the website, you'll find resources to help you build your own Revenue Sourcing map and your own Revenue Sourcing Allocation Plan. You will also find resources to help you maximize the benefits you'll receive from Social Security and be able to request a free fee and drawdown analysis as described in this book.

CHAPTER FIVE

How to Revenue Source Effectively

"Adventure is just bad planning."

– Roald Amundsen

The first two steps of the Revenue Sourcing process are easy. How much retirement income do you need, and when do you want it?

While this can vary from one person to another and their individual circumstances, to get started, assume you want the same level of take-home income that you have presently and then determine the earliest date that you would want to begin receiving this income.

For discussion's sake, let's take the hypothetical example of Frank and Susan. They are both 60 years of age and have determined they will need about $66,000 per year when they retire. That's about their current level of take-home pay after paying taxes and after making their retirement plan contributions in their respective employer's 401(k) plans.

Frank and Susan have decided that they would like to retire in 6 years when they both reach the age of 66.

They have completed the first two steps of the Revenue Sourcing process.

Now, it's time to design the Revenue Sourcing map.

The first thing to do when building the Revenue Sourcing map, as noted in the last chapter, is to figure out the best way to collect Social Security benefits. This topic is a book in and of itself. I wrote a best-selling book on this topic in 2019 titled, "The Little Black Book on Social Security Maximization" that provides a lot of detail on this all-important topic.

For this book, I will cover the most basic of Social Security Maximization strategies. From my experience, most would-be Social Security recipients can use one of these strategies to maximize their Social Security benefits.

It's important to understand that all Social Security collection options are based on two factors, your Primary Insurance Amount and your Normal Retirement Age. Your Primary Insurance

Amount is the full Social Security benefit that you are eligible to collect based upon your own work history. You are eligible to collect this Primary Insurance Amount at your Normal Retirement Age.

Your Normal Retirement Age will vary depending on your birth year.

You can, however, elect to collect your Social Security benefits prior to your Normal Retirement Age. Unless you're disabled, the earliest age at which you can collect Social Security benefits is 62.

Birth Year	Normal Retirement Age
1943–1954	66
1955	66 and 2 months
1956	66 and 4 months
1957	66 and 6 months
1958	66 and 8 months
1959	66 and 10 months

Should you decide to collect Social Security benefits at age 62, the benefit that you collect will be your Primary Insurance Amount discounted by a percentage. The percentage by which your Primary Insurance Amount is discounted will depend on your Normal Retirement Age, as noted by the chart below.

Normal Retirement Age	Discount at 62
66	25%
66 and 2 months	25.83%
66 and 4 months	26.67%
66 and 6 months	27.50%
66 and 8 months	28.33%
66 and 10 months	29.17%
67	30%

For example, if your Primary Insurance Amount is $2,000 per month and your Normal Retirement Age is 66, should you opt to collect Social Security benefits at age 62, your Primary Insurance Amount of $2,000 monthly will be discounted by 25% or $500.

Your choice is to draw $1,500 per month at age 62 or wait and draw $2,000 monthly at your Normal Retirement Age of 66.

What's the best move here?

It depends on your own personal facts and circumstances.

If you're still working and earning a good amount of money, it probably makes sense to wait until your Normal Retirement Age to collect Social Security benefits since there is an earnings limit that could affect the Social Security benefits that you collect prior to your Normal Retirement Age.

In 2020, if you are collecting Social Security benefits and you have not yet reached your Normal Retirement Age, if you earn more than $18,240 in wages, for every $2 you earn over that threshold, you will give up $1 of Social Security benefits.

Let's assume you're 62 and still working, and you earn $40,000 in a year. You want to decide if it makes sense to collect Social Security benefits now, at age 62, or if it makes more sense to wait and collect later, perhaps at your Normal Retirement Age. If you elect to collect Social Security benefits now, you will collect $1,500 per month or $18,000 per year in Social Security benefits. If you're also earning $40,000 per year, you will give up some of your Social Security benefits. Here is the math:

$40,000 earnings - $18,240 earnings limit = $21,760

$21,760 / 2 = $10,880 in Social Security benefits withheld.

In this example, Social Security would withhold ALL benefit payments beginning in January until the forfeited amount is paid, then regular benefit payments would continue for the rest of the year.

At the beginning of each year, Social Security will request that you estimate your income. The withholding for the year will then be based on that estimate. Any discrepancies will be made up in January of the following year after your income has been reported to the IRS.

In the calendar year that you reach your Normal Retirement Age, the earnings test changes and becomes more lenient. If your Normal Retirement Age is 66 in 2020, you can earn up to $48,600 in the months before your birthday and not lose any benefits.

If you earn more than $48,600, you will give up $1 for every $3 in earnings that you have over $48,600.

If you draw Social Security benefits at age 62 and you retire at age 62, earnings prior to your retirement date do not adversely affect your Social Security benefits. Here's an example to make the point clear. A worker turns age 62 on October 30 and retires on her birthday. Prior to retirement on that date, she has earned $50,000. Now, after retirement, the earnings limit applies since she is younger than her Normal Retirement Age; however, the annual earnings limit of $18,240 is prorated monthly to $1,520 ($18,240/12=$1,520). During her first two months of retirement, during the months of November and December, the earnings limit calculation would take place on a monthly basis.

It's important to understand that we're talking about earnings from a job or net self-employment income here. Passive income, like income from investments or retirement accounts, are not included in the formula.

The benefits that are withheld by Social Security while you continue to work are not lost forever. Once you reach your Normal Retirement Age, your monthly benefit will be increased to account for all the months in which benefits were withheld. For example, if you claimed benefits at age 62 but gave up 24 months of benefits over the next four years due to the earnings test, Social Security would adjust your benefit at full retirement age as if you had first claimed at age

64, not age 62 which would give you a higher benefit moving forward.

The earnings test no longer applies when you have attained your Normal Retirement Age.

It's also worth noting here that if a spouse or dependent is drawing Social Security benefits based on your earnings record, those benefits are also withheld while the earnings test is satisfied.

In many cases, if you intend to continue to work and earn a good income, it probably makes sense to consider waiting to collect your Social Security benefits until your Normal Retirement Age at a minimum. But there are always exceptions to the rule.

If you are not planning on working and earning more than the earnings limit, the question is, should you draw Social Security benefits at age 62 or wait until age 66?

When trying to make this decision, many aspiring Social Security program recipients use the term "break-even point." While it is not a technical Social Security term, it's one that practically everyone uses.

Let's calculate the break-even point for Social Security benefits when first collecting benefits at age 62 versus age 66.

In the example above, the age 62 benefit from Social Security is $1,500 per month or $18,000 annually. By drawing Social Security at age 62, one will collect $72,000 by age 66. We'll call that a "head start" amount.

At age 66, the benefit paid by Social Security will be $2,000 monthly or $24,000 per year, or $6,000 more than could be collected at age 62.

The math is straightforward. The head start amount of $72,000 is divided by the additional annual benefit of $6,000; that gives us a "break-even" point of 12 years or age 78 in this example.

Of course, that breakeven point is not indexed for inflation. To be fair when making this calculation, we'd have to assume that a dollar in the future will buy less than a dollar does today. Depending on what inflation factor you want to use, the breakeven point may be further out than age 78, given a dollar collected today from Social Security will probably buy more than a dollar collected at a future point. The reality is the real breakeven point is a bit further out than age 78 in terms of real dollars.

When collecting Social Security, there is also the option of reaching your normal retirement age and then waiting to collect benefits.When you make this decision, the final benefit that you collect from Social Security increases at a rate of .67% per month or 8% per year.

In the example above, assuming a Normal Retirement Age of 66 and a Primary Insurance Amount of $2,000 monthly, for each month that Social Security benefits are deferred, the benefit increases $13.40; if Social Security benefits are deferred for one year, the monthly benefit reaches $2,160.

Social Security benefits can be deferred or delayed until age 70. There is no financial benefit to deferring benefits past age 70. Again, assuming a Normal Retirement Age of 66 and a Primary Insurance Amount of $2,000 monthly, the Primary Insurance Amount Monthly increases by a factor of 32% (8% per year x 4 years) to get the ultimate monthly benefit amount to $2,640 at age 70.

On an annual basis in this example, the Social Security benefit collected at age 66 is $24,000 annually; at age 70, it's $31,680 per year.

Let's walk through the breakeven calculation again.

Drawing Social Security benefits at one's Normal Retirement Age of 66 would mean that by age 70, there was a head start amount collected of $96,000. However, at age 70, the additional annual benefit collected from Social Security will be $7,680 per year. Again, the math is straight forward; the head start amount of $96,000 is divided by the additional annual benefit of $7,680 to determine the breakeven point. ($96,000 head start / $7,680 additional annual benefit = 12.5-year breakeven point)

In this case, drawing Social Security benefits at age 70 versus age 66 has a breakeven point of age 82 1/2 without considering an adjustment for inflation.

Then, assuming earned income is not an issue, there is the comparison of drawing Social Security benefits at age 62 versus age 70.

In this example, annual benefits at age 62 are $18,000, while benefits at age 70 are $31,680 per year. Electing to draw Social Security benefits at age 62 has one drawing total benefits of $144,000, that's the head start amount. At age 70, the additional benefit received per year is $13,680. Once again, we take the head start amount and divide by the additional annual benefit to determine the break-even point.

($144,000 head start / $13,680 additional income = 10.52 years)

The non-inflation adjusted break-even for drawing Social Security benefits at age 62 versus 70 is about age 80 ?.

All of these calculations and outcomes are driven significantly by individual facts and circumstances. There are other factors to consider as well, like eligibility to collect spousal benefits on your spouse or ex-spouse's work history or widow or widower benefits.

When building a Revenue Sourcing map, all of these factors are considered.

The second thing to consider when building your Revenue Sourcing map is whether you will be eligible to collect a traditional, defined benefit pension plan. These are the pension plans that pay you a specified amount each month at a designated age.

While many workers no longer qualify for these plans, if you are among the lucky few that will receive a defined benefit pension plan payout, you should count yourself fortunate.

Most defined benefit pension plans require that a participant select an income option on their plan. Typical choices are a straight life annuity payout or a payout that would pay a survivor all or part of the monthly benefit should the original income beneficiary die before his or her spouse. A straight life annuity pays the worker an income for as long as he or she lives but provides no residual benefit for a surviving spouse. Other collection choices to provide benefits for a surviving spouse.

When constructing a Revenue Sourcing Map, you'll also want to consider earned income. Many people, when retiring, do decide to work part-time or even full-time for some period of time. Others have no plans to retire.

Now that these factors have been determined, we can go back to the first two big questions:

1.) How much income do you desire during retirement?

2.) When do you want to get that income?

Subtracting income from Social Security, pension, and earned income from the total desired income will help us determine how much income we will need to withdraw from our investments.

We are now ready to build our Revenue Sourcing Map.

Revenue Sourcing Resources

Visit www.Revenue-Sourcing.com
for additional Revenue Sourcing resources.

Our team hosts periodic, free webinars on how you can use Revenue Sourcing to achieve your dream of a comfortable, stress-free retirement. Also, on the website, you'll find resources to help you build your own Revenue Sourcing map and your own Revenue Sourcing Allocation Plan. You will also find resources to help you maximize the benefits you'll receive from Social Security and be able to request a free fee and drawdown analysis as described in this book.

CHAPTER SIX
Revenue Sourcing Case Study

*"Good plans shape good decisions.
That's why good planning helps make elusive
dreams come true."*

– Lester R. Bittel

In this chapter, we will review a hypothetical Revenue Sourcing case study. Keep in mind that Revenue Sourcing is a process. The four steps of the Revenue Sourcing process are:

1.) Identify the level of retirement income needed or desired.

2.) Identify when the income will be needed.

3.) Build the Revenue Sourcing Map. Include Social Security income, pension income, earned income, business income, and income from investments.

4.) Once the Revenue Sourcing Map is built, adjust allocations, and do long-term tax management.

Let's consider the example of Frank and Susan. They are both 60 years of age and plan to retire in 6 years when they attain age 66. They have done some preliminary planning and determined that they would like to have $66,000 annually when they retire, which would be the equivalent after-tax income of their current $102,000 gross.

They are presently contributing $20,000 per year to retirement accounts out of their gross income of $102,000. They are paying Medicare and Social Security tax of about $7,800 annually. In addition, Federal tax liability on an annual basis is about $9,000, and their state tax liability is about $3,200.

At retirement in 6 years, Frank and Susan will no longer be contributing to their respective 401(k) plans, will cease paying Social Security tax, and the Social Security benefits they receive will be largely non-taxable. Total tax liability will be less than $200 annually. This will give Frank and Susan a slightly more spendable income during retirement than they had when they were working.

Frank is contributing $12,000 per year to his 401(k) plan, which has a current account balance of $485,000 after a recent decline and rebound in the investments he holds in his account.

Susan's 401(k) has an account balance of $279,000, and she is contributing $8,000 per year to her account. Susan's account balance is also down fairly significantly from her peak account balance.

Frank and Susan have completed the first two steps of the Revenue Sourcing process. Step One – determine how much income they'll desire at retirement.In Frank and Susan's case, the amount is $66,000 per year. Step Two – determine when they will want to get the income. In their case, the income needs to begin in 6 years when they plan to retire.

The next step in the Revenue Sourcing process is to do a Social Security Maximization analysis. After doing a thorough analysis, it was determined that Frank and Susan should collect Social Security benefits when they retire at age 66. (Note: If you would like to obtain a complete Social Security analysis for your personal situation, visit www.SocialSecurityMaximizationReport.com and request it.)

Frank and Susan

Age at Year End			Assumed Annual Additions	$12,000	$8,000	
			Present Balance	$485,000	$279,000	$764,000
			Assumed Growth Rate	4%	4%	4%
			Account Type	401(k)	401(k)	
	Frank	Susan		Frank	Susan	Total Retirement Assets
2020	60	60		$508,550	$293,370	$801,920
2021	61	61		$540,892	$313,105	$853,997
2022	62	62		$574,528	$325,629	$900,157
2023	63	63		$597,509	$338,654	$936,163
2024	64	64		$621,409	$352,200	$973,609
2025	65	65		$646,266	$366,288	$1,012,554
2026	66	66				$1,017,609
2027	67	67				$1,058,314
2028	68	68				$1,080,146
2029	69	69				$1,102,852
2030	70	70				$1,126,466
2031	71	71				$1,151,025
2032	72	72				$1,176,566
2033	73	73				$1,203,128
2034	74	74				$1,230,754
2035	75	75				$1,259,484
2036	76	76				$1,289,363
2037	77	77				$1,320,438
2038	78	78				$1,352,755
2039	79	79				$1,386,365
2040	80	80				$1,421,320
2041	81	81				$1,457,673
2042	82	82				$1,495,480
2043	83	83				$1,534,799
2044	84	84				$1,575,691
2045	85	85				$1,618,218
2046	86	86				$1,662,447
2047	87	87				$1,708,445
2048	88	88				$1,756,283
2049	89	89				$1,806,034
2050	90	90				$1,857,775
2051	91	91				$1,911,587
2052	92	92				$1,967,550
2053	93	93				$2,025,752
2054	94	94				$2,086,282
2055	95	95				$2,149,233
2056	96	96				$2,214,703
2057	97	97				$2,282,791
2058	98	98				$2,353,602

For discussion only. These hypothetical projections should not be considered a solicitation to buy or sell any asset. This is not investment advice. These projections contains many assumptions, including but not limited to assumed growth rates, asset balances, spending, and tax laws.

Revenue Sourcing Model

Earned Income	Frank's Social Security	Susan's Social Security	Withdrawls Retirement Assests	Total Income
$102,000				$102,000
$102,000				$102,000
$102,000				$102,000
$102,000				$102,000
$102,000				$102,000
$102,000				$102,000
$0	$22,917	$9,000	$34,083	$66,000
$0	$27,500	$18,000	$20,500	$66,000
$0	$27,500	$18,000	$20,500	$66,000
$0	$27,500	$18,000	$20,500	$66,000
$0	$27,500	$18,000	$20,500	$66,000
$0	$27,500	$18,000	$20,500	$66,000
$0	$27,500	$18,000	$20,500	$66,000
$0	$27,500	$18,000	$20,500	$66,000
$0	$27,500	$18,000	$20,500	$66,000
$0	$27,500	$18,000	$20,500	$66,000
$0	$27,500	$18,000	$20,500	$66,000
$0	$27,500	$18,000	$20,500	$66,000
$0	$27,500	$18,000	$20,500	$66,000
$0	$27,500	$18,000	$20,500	$66,000
$0	$27,500	$18,000	$20,500	$66,000
$0	$27,500	$18,000	$20,500	$66,000
$0	$27,500	$18,000	$20,500	$66,000
$0	$27,500	$18,000	$20,500	$66,000
$0	$27,500	$18,000	$20,500	$66,000
$0	$27,500	$18,000	$20,500	$66,000
$0	$27,500	$18,000	$20,500	$66,000
$0	$27,500	$18,000	$20,500	$66,000
$0	$27,500	$18,000	$20,500	$66,000
$0	$27,500	$18,000	$20,500	$66,000
$0	$27,500	$18,000	$20,500	$66,000
$0	$27,500	$18,000	$20,500	$66,000
$0	$27,500	$18,000	$20,500	$66,000
$0	$27,500	$18,000	$20,500	$66,000
$0	$27,500	$18,000	$20,500	$66,000

Neither Frank or Susan will be eligible to collect a traditional, defined benefit pension plan when they retire, and neither plan on any earned income once they reach age 66 and retire.

Frank will receive Social Security benefits of $27,500 per year at age 66, while Susan will collect $18,000 annually. That will provide Frank and Susan with annual benefits from Social Security of $45,500.

Since their income goal will be $66,000 per year at retirement, Frank and Susan will need to pull $20,400 per year from their investments to meet their income desires. Here is Frank and Susan's Revenue Sourcing Map, on pages 88-89.

Age at Year End	Frank	Susan
	Assumed Annual Additions	
	Present Balance	
	Assumed Growth Rate	
	Account Type	
2020	60	60
2021	61	61
2022	62	62
2023	63	63
2024	64	64
2025	65	65
2026	66	66
2027	67	67
2028	68	68
2029	69	69
2030	70	70
2031	71	71
2032	72	72
2033	73	73
2034	74	74
2035	75	75
2036	76	76
2037	77	77
2038	78	78
2039	79	79
2040	80	80
2041	81	81
2042	82	82
2043	83	83
2044	84	84
2045	85	85
2046	86	86
2047	87	87
2048	88	88
2049	89	89
2050	90	90
2051	91	91
2052	92	92
2053	93	93
2054	94	94
2055	95	95
2056	96	96
2057	97	97
2058	98	98

Frank and Susan's Revenue Sourcing Map is broken down into three different sections. The left-hand side of the Revenue Sourcing Map (the area to the left of the vertical line that is farthest left identifies time frames. The area between the two bold vertical lines illustrates investment assets. The area on the far right of the chart illustrates total retirement assets and then income sources.

I'll break down each section for you.

First, the time frames section. This section is straightforward. It illustrates Frank and Susan's age at the end of each calendar year.

At the end of the calendar year 2020, both Frank and Susan will be

$12,000	$8,000
$485,000	$279,000
4%	4%
401(k)	401(k)
Frank	Susan
$508,550	$293,370
$540,892	$313,105
$574,528	$325,629
$597,509	$338,654
$621,409	$352,200
$646,266	$366,288

60 years of age. The time frames part of Frank and Susan's Revenue Sourcing map runs out to the calendar year 2058 when they are both 98 years of age.

The next section of the Revenue Sourcing map, the center section, illustrates Frank and Susan's investments. Like many career workers, both Frank and Susan have a 401(k) plan to which they contribute and to which their respective employers add a matching contribution.

This "investments" section illustrates the current balance of Frank and Susan's 401(k) plan as well as the combined employer and employee ongoing contribution to the plan.

In Frank's case, as noted from the investments section on the Revenue

Sourcing Map, his current 401(k) plan balance
is $485,000, and he and his employer will con-
tribute $12,000 per year to his plan. Susan's
401(k) has an account balance of $279,000, and
between her contribution and her employer's
match, a total of $8,000 per year will be added
to her account.

You'll note on the investments section of the
Revenue Sourcing Map that we are building the
map based on a growth assumption of 4% annually. It's important to note that this is not a return
goal or objective, merely a growth assumption
intentionally designed to be conservative.

When it comes to assumptions, my experience in the financial industry has taught me that
assumptions are always wrong. In most cases,
they're too optimistic. Using assumptions that
are too rosy or overly enthusiastic can be the
death of a solid Revenue Sourcing plan. It's best
to use assumptions that are too conservative.
If a Revenue Sourcing Map will deliver desired
outcomes using assumptions that are too conservative, then the probability of success is high.

This requires a mindset shift for many aspiring
retirees.

The reality is, many who aspire to a comfortable, stress-free retirement don't have goals, or

they have goals that are incongruent with their real desire. The Revenue Sourcing process will help an aspiring retiree align their plan with their real goals.

This goes back to using strategies, as I discussed at the beginning of this book. Many financial professionals don't use strategies because they don't take time to understand and clearly define investment goals.

When you approach retirement, your perspective must change. Your investment returns are not as important as having your assets positioned in such a way as to allow you to achieve and enjoy the lifestyle about which you've always dreamed.

The last section of the Revenue Sourcing Map is the income portion. This is the section that has the most moving parts. It illustrates total investment assets and anticipated retirement income. Retirement income can come from Social Security, pension income, earned income, inheritance income, or income from investments.

In the case of Frank and Susan, after conducting a Social Security maximization analysis, we determined that they should draw Social Security as soon as they retire.As a reminder, a Social Security maximization study examines all collection options, including spousal benefits (if eligible), options to suspend benefits to allow for an increase in the level of benefits, and different collection dates. A Social Security maximization analysis is one of the core elements of the Revenue Sourcing Map.

In Frank and Susan's case, they are not eligible for a defined benefit pension plan, nor do they anticipate any earned income during retirement. They are also not anticipating an inheritance that would greatly influence their net worth.

Frank and Susan's Revenue Sourcing Map is simple. They will receive combined annual benefits from Social Security of $45,500 and will need to withdraw $20,500 per year from their investments each year.

Frank and Susan's Revenue Sourcing Map illustrates these income streams.

On the income portion of the Revenue Sourcing Map, the first column, moving left to the right, is the "Total Retirement Assets" column. This is the combined total of Frank and Susan's retirement account assets, growing at our conservative growth assumption of 4%.

$764,000					
4%					

Total Retirement Assets	Earned Income	Frank's Social Security	Susan's Social Security	Withdrawls Retirement Assests	Total Income
$801,920	$102,000				$102,000
$853,997	$102,000				$102,000
$900,157	$102,000				$102,000
$936,163	$102,000				$102,000
$973,609	$102,000				$102,000
$1,012,554	$102,000				$102,000
$1,017,609	$0	$22,917	$9,000	$34,083	$66,000
$1,058,314	$0	$27,500	$18,000	$20,500	$66,000
$1,080,146	$0	$27,500	$18,000	$20,500	$66,000
$1,102,852	$0	$27,500	$18,000	$20,500	$66,000
$1,126,466	$0	$27,500	$18,000	$20,500	$66,000
$1,151,025	$0	$27,500	$18,000	$20,500	$66,000
$1,176,566	$0	$27,500	$18,000	$20,500	$66,000
$1,203,128	$0	$27,500	$18,000	$20,500	$66,000
$1,230,754	$0	$27,500	$18,000	$20,500	$66,000
$1,259,484	$0	$27,500	$18,000	$20,500	$66,000
$1,289,363	$0	$27,500	$18,000	$20,500	$66,000
$1,320,438	$0	$27,500	$18,000	$20,500	$66,000
$1,352,755	$0	$27,500	$18,000	$20,500	$66,000
$1,386,365	$0	$27,500	$18,000	$20,500	$66,000
$1,421,320	$0	$27,500	$18,000	$20,500	$66,000
$1,457,673	$0	$27,500	$18,000	$20,500	$66,000
$1,495,480	$0	$27,500	$18,000	$20,500	$66,000
$1,534,799	$0	$27,500	$18,000	$20,500	$66,000
$1,575,691	$0	$27,500	$18,000	$20,500	$66,000
$1,618,218	$0	$27,500	$18,000	$20,500	$66,000
$1,662,447	$0	$27,500	$18,000	$20,500	$66,000
$1,708,445	$0	$27,500	$18,000	$20,500	$66,000
$1,756,283	$0	$27,500	$18,000	$20,500	$66,000
$1,806,034	$0	$27,500	$18,000	$20,500	$66,000
$1,857,775	$0	$27,500	$18,000	$20,500	$66,000
$1,911,587	$0	$27,500	$18,000	$20,500	$66,000
$1,967,550	$0	$27,500	$18,000	$20,500	$66,000
$2,025,752	$0	$27,500	$18,000	$20,500	$66,000
$2,086,282	$0	$27,500	$18,000	$20,500	$66,000
$2,149,233	$0	$27,500	$18,000	$20,500	$66,000
$2,214,703	$0	$27,500	$18,000	$20,500	$66,000
$2,282,791	$0	$27,500	$18,000	$20,500	$66,000
$2,353,602	$0	$27,500	$18,000	$20,500	$66,000

Moving further to the right across the income portion of the Revenue Sourcing Map, we see Frank and Susan's combined earned income of $102,000 annually that ceases six years in when Frank and Susan both retire.

As noted above, Frank and Susan are not eligible to receive a traditional defined benefit pension, nor are they expecting an inheritance or income from any other source, so on Frank and Susan's Revenue Sourcing Map, we are illustrating only Social Security benefits and Withdrawals from Retirement Assets.

There is a column on the Revenue Sourcing Map labeled "Withdrawals Retirement Assets." That column shows the withdrawals from investment assets that are required to reach Frank and Susan's income goals of $66,000 per year. These withdrawals are subtracted from the "Total Retirement Assets" column that is growing at 4%.

Note from the Revenue Sourcing Map that this is an achievable plan for Frank and Susan.

To use a sports analogy, we have drawn up the game plan for Frank and Susan, and it looks good on paper. But, as any sports fan knows, a game plan is only as good as it's execution. That's the topic of the next chapter.

Revenue Sourcing Resources

Visit www.Revenue-Sourcing.com
for additional Revenue Sourcing resources.

Our team hosts periodic, free webinars on how you can use Revenue Sourcing to achieve your dream of a comfortable, stress-free retirement. Also, on the website, you'll find resources to help you build your own Revenue Sourcing map and your own Revenue Sourcing Allocation Plan. You will also find resources to help you maximize the benefits you'll receive from Social Security and be able to request a free fee and drawdown analysis as described in this book.

CHAPTER SEVEN

Revenue Sourcing Implementation – Part One

"That is the greatest fallacy, the wisdom of old men. They do not grow wise; they grow careful."

– Ernest Hemmingway

To effectively execute your Revenue Sourcing Map, you need to be careful to avoid anything that could 'blow up' your Revenue Sourcing Map.

In this chapter, we'll look at one obstacle that could totally destroy your Revenue Sourcing Map and another that can have a big impact.

The first and most dangerous of these obstacles is drawdown.

It's a term not often discussed by financial professionals. You have probably never even heard of it.

And, that's a shame because drawdown has proven fatal to more retirement plans than any other factor.

While much of the financial industry is talking about average annual return and encouraging investors and would-be retirees to chase yields, the number one topic of conversation should be drawdown.

Let me let you in on a little industry secret. Average annual yield is an overused performance metric that can be terribly misleading. Let me give you an example by asking a simple question.

Would you prefer an investment that gave you a 0% net return or a 25% average annual return?

OK, you caught me. It's a trick question.

They can be the same investment.

Let's assume you have an investment account with a balance of $100,000, and you experience a 50% annual decline. You now have an account with $50,000 in it. The next year your investment enjoys a 100% gain. You are now back to your original account balance of $100,000.

Now, for discussion's sake, over the next two years, let's assume that the investment performance repeats. In year three, your investment experiences a 50% decline, and in year four, you get another 100% gain.

At the end of four years, you've experienced a 0% net return. But, the same four years have you experiencing an average annual return of 25%. Here's the math:

Year One	- 50%
Year Two	+100%
Year Three	- 50%
Year Four	+100%
Total	100% divided by four years = 25% average annual return

This simple example demonstrates why looking at average annual return alone can be misleading. A better investment statistic to consider is drawdown.

Drawdown is defined as the distance between an investment peak or high point and its trough or low point. A chart best illustrates it.

This chart is a price chart of the Standard and Poor's 500 during the bust cycle of 2007-2009. Notice that from peak to the trough, stocks fell more than 53%.

Here's why that is so important. For every percentage loss an investor experiences in his or her portfolio, the percentage gain subsequent to the loss experienced must be exponentially greater.

In other words, percentage losses hurt a portfolio more than a percentage gain helps it.

This relationship between percentage losses and percentage gains is often explained by the 'break-even curve.' This curve illustrates the exponential relationship between portfolio percentage losses and portfolio percentage gains.

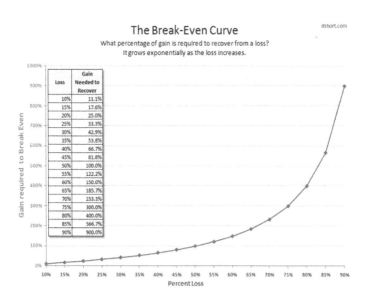

The Break-Even Curve

øshort.com

What percentage of gain is required to recover from a loss?
It grows exponentially as the loss increases.

Loss	Gain Needed to Recover
10%	11.1%
15%	17.6%
20%	25.0%
25%	33.3%
30%	42.9%
35%	53.8%
40%	66.7%
45%	81.8%
50%	100.0%
55%	122.2%
60%	150.0%
65%	185.7%
70%	233.3%
75%	300.0%
80%	400.0%
85%	566.7%
90%	900.0%

Notice from the chart that a 10% loss requires an 11% gain to get back to even.

A 50% loss requires a 100% gain to get back to the starting point, and a 90% loss requires a 900% gain to return to square one.

As I write this, stocks corrected top to bottom about 30% after the coronavirus economic constraints were put in place. Undoubtedly, things will have changed significantly with regard to stocks by the time you read this.

The Federal Reserve, as noted previously, is pulling out all the stops, frantically trying to reflate the bubble. If they're successful, the next bust cycle will be even more painful.

If the Fed is not successful, the bust that began with the coronavirus economic constraints will continue and will likely get a lot worse, subjecting many aspiring retirees to levels of drawdown never previously experienced.

Here is why I come to that conclusion.

Even after the most recent drawdown in stocks, stock valuations fell back to the level at which the 2007 decline began. Let me be clear here. Even after stocks fell more than 30% from recent highs, valuations were at the same level as when the prior bust cycle began.

To reach this conclusion, I use Warren Buffet's favorite stock valuation measure, which is total market capitalization to gross domestic product.

Total market capitalization is the total value of all stocks. To calculate total market capitalization, one would take all shares of stock in existence and multiply by the share price of each share of stock.

Then, by adding together the total value of all stocks, you come up with total market capitalization.

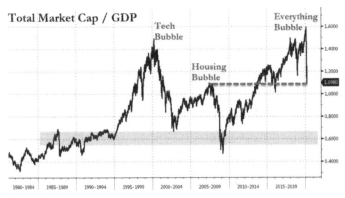

Source: Bloomberg

Gross domestic product is the total value of all goods and services produced within a country's borders. In other words, gross domestic product, or GDP is the total economic output.

Taking total market capitalization and dividing by gross domestic product gives you the ratio that can help determine if stocks are overvalued or are undervalued.

Notice from the chart that was produced at the recent stock market bottom that the market capitalization to gross domestic product ratio got stock valuations back to where the decline began in 2007.

It's important to note that stocks fell more than 53% from these valuation levels in 2007 during the Great Recession. And it's also important to note that the biggest quarterly decline in gross domestic product during that time frame was 8.4%.

GDP decline is projected to be 30% to 50% moving ahead. Some big Wall Street banks are forecasting a decline of up to 30% while James Bullard, the president of the St; Louis Federal Reserve Bank, estimates GDP could take a hit of up to 50%.

Should that occur and should the headline unemployment rate jump to 20% or 25% as seems likely, stocks will not react favorably. I'd suggest that a 50% to 80% decline in stocks from the recent lows is possible.

That would put the Dow Jones Industrial Average somewhere between 5,000 and 9,000 as unrealistic as that may sound presently. In my "New Retirement Rules" book, I forecast a Dow to Gold ratio of 2, or more likely 1. That means by taking the value of the Dow and dividing by the price of gold per ounce in US Dollars, you come up with a number of 1 or 2.

This is another compelling reason to use Revenue Sourcing. If my forecast is correct, Revenue Sourcing could preserve a comfortable financial future for you. If my forecast is wrong and stocks don't fall as far as my models predict, you can still preserve a comfortable financial future; you'll potentially just miss some upside return.

Isn't that a better mistake to make?

Doesn't it make more sense to miss some upside than risk participating in a downside that has the potential to be more devastating than 1929?

That's why Revenue Sourcing has been developed.

There is also another potential benefit to using Revenue Sourcing.

As your Revenue Sourcing Map is designed, an analysis of your existing holdings is done. During this analysis, the level of fees that you are paying to investment companies and financial professionals is examined. Many investors, as a result of this analysis, conclude they are overpaying on fees.

This review of existing investments also includes an analysis of historical drawdown. What is the worst year that your existing investment has had? What level of drawdown has been experienced?

While past performance is not necessarily indicative of future performance, this data is valuable.

This chart is a chart of a fee and drawdown analysis that my team did for an aspiring retiree.

Fund Name	Value	Total	Exisiting Fees	ETF Fees	Worst 12 Month Return as %	Worst 12 Month Return in Dollars
Fund A	$38,577	$38,577	$467	$37	-49.55%	-$19,115
Fund B	$21,508	$21,508	$88	$25	4.83%	-$1,039
Fund C	$50,134	$50,134	$431	$49	45.33%	-$22,726
Fund D	$31,750	$31,750	$248	$42	11.70%	-$3,715
Fund E	$24,732	$24,732	$270	$23	34.34%	-$8,493
Fund F	$31,753	$31,753	$286	$31	35.90%	-$11,399
Fund G	$21,087	$21,087	$224	$20	33.87%	-$7,142
Fund H	$18,772	$18,772	$139	$20	6.92%	-$1,299
Fund I	$22,642	$22,642	$168	$24	26.22%	-$5,937
Fund J	$25,487	$25,487	$273	$26	21.36%	-$5,444
Fund K	$29,649	$29,649	$122	$32	6.84%	-$2,028
Fund L	$12,760	$12,760	$88	$13	40.79%	-$5,205
Fund M	$10,678	$10,678	$111	$11	54.66%	-$5,837
Fund N	$46,134	$46,134	$346	$53	17.05%	-$7,866
Fund O	$19,471	$19,471	$90	$26	3.60%	-$701
Fund P	$63,486	$63,486	$489	$63	43.90%	-$27,870
Fund Q	$39,784	$39,784	$565	$37	50.96%	-$20,274
	$508,404	Total Fees	$4,402	$531	Total	-$156,089

While we've hidden the name of the funds owned by this investor and the fund symbol, we have included the portfolio balance, existing fees, comparable fees an investor might pay in an exchange-traded fund as well as drawdown on a percentage basis and in terms of dollars based on the present account balance.

Notice that this portfolio has a balance of about $508,000. That may seem like a small portfolio to you, or perhaps it seems large. It really doesn't matter, just move the decimal in either direction to make this example more realistic for your individual situation.

Total current fees being paid internally on this portfolio are approximately $4,400 per year. An examination of low-cost alternatives to the funds presently owned found that fees could potentially be reduced to a little more than $500. That's possible savings of $3,900 per year. Over the course of a 30-year retirement, that can really add up; nearly $120,000 in excess fees in this hypothetical example.

It's important to note that the fees may not stop there. Often, an investor pays a financial professional to help them choose their investments. While the fees a financial professional may charge for this service vary, an annual fee of 1% is not unusual. If that was the case in this situation, total fees could exceed $9,000 per year.

It's important to remember that money managers and advisors get paid before you do. And, money managers and advisors get paid whether your account is going up in value or is going down in value.

If you can reduce fees and get an outcome you like, you'll keep more of your money.

Revenue Sourcing Resources

Visit www.Revenue-Sourcing.com
for additional Revenue Sourcing resources.

Our team hosts periodic, free webinars on how you can use Revenue Sourcing to achieve your dream of a comfortable, stress-free retirement. Also, on the website, you'll find resources to help you build your own Revenue Sourcing map and your own Revenue Sourcing Allocation Plan. You will also find resources to help you maximize the benefits you'll receive from Social Security and be able to request a free fee and drawdown analysis as described in this book.

CHAPTER EIGHT

Revenue Sourcing Implementation – Part Two

"Knowledge speaks, but wisdom listens."

– Jimi Hendrix

Once you've done your fee and drawdown analysis, your Social Security Maximization analysis, and then built your Revenue Sourcing Map, it's time for the last step in the Revenue Sourcing process. It's time to build a Revenue Sourcing Allocation Model.

This is the simplest part of the Revenue Sourcing process.

And, the concept is simple. Get the assets that you'll need to produce your desired retirement income to a vehicle that is safe and stable and reserve the balance of the assets to be invested for an inflation hedge.

Let's go back and review Frank and Susan's situation again.

After completing their Revenue Sourcing Map, they needed to have income from their investments, as noted from the chart on this page, reprinted again from Chapter Six.

$764,000					
4%					

Total Retirement Assets	Earned Income	Frank's Social Security	Susan's Social Security	Withdrawls Retirement Assests	Total Income
$801,920	$102,000				$102,000
$853,997	$102,000				$102,000
$900,157	$102,000				$102,000
$936,163	$102,000				$102,000
$973,609	$102,000				$102,000
$1,012,554	$102,000				$102,000
$1,017,609	$0	$22,917	$9,000	$34,083	$66,000
$1,058,314	$0	$27,500	$18,000	$20,500	$66,000
$1,080,146	$0	$27,500	$18,000	$20,500	$66,000
$1,102,852	$0	$27,500	$18,000	$20,500	$66,000
$1,126,466	$0	$27,500	$18,000	$20,500	$66,000
$1,151,025	$0	$27,500	$18,000	$20,500	$66,000
$1,176,566	$0	$27,500	$18,000	$20,500	$66,000
$1,203,128	$0	$27,500	$18,000	$20,500	$66,000
$1,230,754	$0	$27,500	$18,000	$20,500	$66,000
$1,259,484	$0	$27,500	$18,000	$20,500	$66,000
$1,289,363	$0	$27,500	$18,000	$20,500	$66,000
$1,320,438	$0	$27,500	$18,000	$20,500	$66,000
$1,352,755	$0	$27,500	$18,000	$20,500	$66,000
$1,386,365	$0	$27,500	$18,000	$20,500	$66,000
$1,421,320	$0	$27,500	$18,000	$20,500	$66,000
$1,457,673	$0	$27,500	$18,000	$20,500	$66,000
$1,495,480	$0	$27,500	$18,000	$20,500	$66,000
$1,534,799	$0	$27,500	$18,000	$20,500	$66,000
$1,575,691	$0	$27,500	$18,000	$20,500	$66,000
$1,618,218	$0	$27,500	$18,000	$20,500	$66,000
$1,662,447	$0	$27,500	$18,000	$20,500	$66,000
$1,708,445	$0	$27,500	$18,000	$20,500	$66,000
$1,756,283	$0	$27,500	$18,000	$20,500	$66,000
$1,806,034	$0	$27,500	$18,000	$20,500	$66,000
$1,857,775	$0	$27,500	$18,000	$20,500	$66,000
$1,911,587	$0	$27,500	$18,000	$20,500	$66,000
$1,967,550	$0	$27,500	$18,000	$20,500	$66,000
$2,025,752	$0	$27,500	$18,000	$20,500	$66,000
$2,086,282	$0	$27,500	$18,000	$20,500	$66,000
$2,149,233	$0	$27,500	$18,000	$20,500	$66,000
$2,214,703	$0	$27,500	$18,000	$20,500	$66,000
$2,282,791	$0	$27,500	$18,000	$20,500	$66,000
$2,353,602	$0	$27,500	$18,000	$20,500	$66,000

Notice that in year seven of the Revenue Sourcing Map that Frank and Susan will require $34,083 in withdrawals from their investments, and beginning in year 8, they will withdraw $20,500 per year.

The Revenue Sourcing Allocation Model will have Frank and Susan earmark or set aside enough of their investment assets in something safe and stable to meet their income needs for the rest of their life.

By setting aside some assets in a vehicle that is safe and stable, Frank and Susan can rest easy knowing that when the stock market crashes in the next bust cycle, the assets that they will rely on for income won't be affected by drawdown.

As mentioned, this is accomplished in the Revenue Sourcing system by dividing assets into two 'buckets' of money, as noted by the chart on pages 114-115.

The first bucket of assets is the "Stable Assets" bucket. These are assets that will be needed to meet the income needs of Frank and Susan. Frank and Susan's Revenue Sourcing Map has them depositing $350,000 in the Stable Assets bucket.

You can see all the income that Frank and Susan will need from their investments based on

Frank and Susan

	Stable Assets - Source of Needed Revenues				
	Initial Deposit:	$350,000			
	Growth Rate:	2%	3%	4%	5%
Year	Income				
1	$0	$350,000	$350,000	$350,000	$350,000
2	$0	$357,000	$360,500	$364,000	$367,500
3	$0	$364,140	$371,315	$378,560	$385,875
4	$0	$371,423	$382,454	$393,702	$405,169
5	$0	$378,851	$393,928	$409,450	$425,427
6	$0	$386,428	$405,746	$425,829	$446,699
7	$34,083	$394,157	$417,918	$442,862	$469,033
8	$20,500	$367,275	$395,350	$425,130	$456,698
9	$20,500	$353,711	$386,096	$420,815	$458,008
10	$20,500	$339,875	$376,564	$416,328	$459,383
11	$20,500	$325,763	$366,746	$411,661	$460,827
12	$20,500	$311,368	$356,633	$406,807	$462,344
13	$20,500	$296,685	$346,217	$401,759	$463,936
14	$20,500	$281,709	$335,489	$396,510	$465,608
15	$20,500	$266,433	$324,438	$391,050	$467,363
16	$20,500	$250,852	$313,056	$385,372	$469,206
17	$20,500	$234,959	$301,333	$379,467	$471,142
18	$20,500	$218,748	$289,258	$373,326	$473,174
19	$20,500	$202,213	$276,821	$366,939	$475,307
20	$20,500	$185,347	$264,010	$360,296	$477,548
21	$20,500	$168,144	$250,816	$353,388	$479,900
22	$20,500	$150,597	$237,225	$346,204	$482,370
23	$20,500	$132,699	$223,227	$338,732	$484,964
24	$20,500	$114,443	$208,809	$330,961	$487,687
25	$20,500	$95,822	$193,958	$322,880	$490,546
26	$20,500	$76,828	$178,662	$314,475	$493,549

their Revenue Sourcing Map for the rest of their life will be taken from the Stable Assets bucket. Beginning in year seven, Frank and Susan will draw $34,083 from the Stable Assets bucket, and then beginning in year eight, the withdrawal needed will be $20,500 annually.

Revenue Sourcing Allocation

Assets to Protect Against Future Inflation			
Initial Deposit:	$414,000		
4%	6%	8%	Annual
Year			Additions
1	$429,000	$429,000	$429,000	$15,000
2	$466,160	$474,740	$483,320	$20,000
3	$504,806	$523,224	$541,986	$20,000
4	$544,999	$574,618	$605,344	$20,000
5	$586,799	$629,095	$673,772	$20,000
6	$630,271	$686,841	$747,674	$20,000
7	$655,481	$728,051	$807,488	$0
8	$681,701	$771,734	$872,087	$0
9	$708,969	$818,038	$941,854	$0
10	$737,327	$867,120	$1,017,202	$0
11	$766,820	$919,148	$1,098,578	$0
12	$797,493	$974,297	$1,186,464	$0
13	$829,393	$1,032,754	$1,281,381	$0
14	$862,569	$1,094,720	$1,383,892	$0
15	$897,072	$1,160,403	$1,494,603	$0
16	$932,954	$1,230,027	$1,614,172	$0
17	$970,273	$1,303,829	$1,743,305	$0
18	$1,009,083	$1,382,058	$1,882,770	$0
19	$1,049,447	$1,464,982	$2,033,391	$0
20	$1,091,425	$1,552,881	$2,196,063	$0
21	$1,135,082	$1,646,054	$2,371,748	$0
22	$1,180,485	$1,744,817	$2,561,487	$0
23	$1,227,704	$1,849,506	$2,766,406	$0
24	$1,276,812	$1,960,476	$2,987,719	$0
25	$1,327,885	$2,078,105	$3,226,736	$0
26	$1,381,000	$2,202,791	$3,484,875	$0

Again, the strategy here is to avoid the bust cycle with these assets.

Notice that in the Stable Assets bucket, we are illustrating four different, annualized rates of return – 2%, 3%, 4%, and 5%. Even with a 2% rate of return, Frank and Susan will be able to meet their income needs. Twenty-six years out, when Frank and Susan reach age 86, assuming just a 2% return on assets. With a 4% return on assets, Frank and Susan still have $314,475 in the Stable Assets bucket at their age 86.

Frank and Susan's other assets, in this case, $414,000, are invested to protect against future inflation. Given today's monetary policy of massive levels of money printing, it's only a matter of time before an inflation hedge will probably be needed.

I believe that using this allocation approach – one Stable Assets bucket of money and one Inflation Hedge bucket of money – will be essential for financial success given the current unprecedented environment and policy response.

The next logical question is, how do you invest the Stable Assets bucket of money and how do you invest the Inflation Hedge bucket of money.

While the answer to that all-important question will vary, depending on each person's individual financial situation, there are some constants from one person to the next given the current environment.

The Stable Assets bucket should never be invested in stock funds or bond funds. Stock funds will decline when stocks fall. Subjecting money in the Stable Assets bucket to stock market risk defeats the purpose of using the two-bucket approach. Bond funds should also be avoided in the Stable Assets bucket. In a climate of rising interest rates, bond funds can lose just as much money as stock funds.

Assets in the Stable Asset bucket should be invested for stability first and foremost. Return potential should be a secondary consideration for Stable Assets.

The Inflation Hedge bucket of money should be invested in such a manner as to perform well in an inflationary environment. These assets should be assets that preserve purchasing power in an inflationary cycle. In other words, these assets should increase in value by some multiple of the dollar's diminishing purchasing power. If the dollar's purchasing power declines on a real basis by 5%, the assets in the Inflation Hedge bucket of money should increase on a real basis by more than 5%.

If you'd like to learn more about Revenue Sourcing and how to adapt it to your own personal situation, visit www.Revenue-Sourcing. com. On that website, you will find additional resources.

You will find an invitation to attend periodic free educational webinars to help you learn more about using Revenue Sourcing in your personal situation.

We live in difficult and unprecedented times. Using traditional planning strategies to plan for your retirement will likely not get you where you want to be. A new planning environment requires new methodologies to help you succeed.

I sincerely hope that this book has offered you a valuable perspective. I leave you with a quote from Eric Hoffer:

"In times of drastic change, it is the learners who inherit the future. The learned find themselves beautifully equipped to live in a world that no longer exists."

Revenue Sourcing Resources

Visit www.Revenue-Sourcing.com
for additional Revenue Sourcing resources.

Our team hosts periodic, free webinars on how you can use Revenue Sourcing to achieve your dream of a comfortable, stress-free retirement. Also, on the website, you'll find resources to help you build your own Revenue Sourcing map and your own Revenue Sourcing Allocation Plan. You will also find resources to help you maximize the benefits you'll receive from Social Security and be able to request a free fee and drawdown analysis as described in this book.

REVENUE SOURCING

Made in the USA
Middletown, DE
27 July 2020